WELSH
n i c k n a m e s

D1643372

WELSH
nicknames

Les Chamberlain

First impression: 2013

© Copyright Les Chamberlain and Y Lolfa Cyf., 2013

Cartoons: Mick Davis

Cover design: Y Lolfa

ISBN: 978 184771 652 1

FSC

Published and printed in Wales
on paper from well maintained forests by
Y Lolfa Cyf., Talybont, Ceredigion SY24 5HE
website www.ylolfa.com
e-mail ylolfa@ylolfa.com
tel 01970 832 304
fax 832 782

Introduction

Nicknames are nothing new. Look back at Bible times and you have Doubting Thomas, Simon the Zealot, Peter the Big Fisherman, James and John Boanerges – Sons of Thunder – and Herod the Great.

But how did nicknames come to be given in Britain? There are a number of theories, but probably the most authentic is that of primitive man's habit of regarding his real name as his very own property and so, rarely, if ever, to be used. To his companions he was therefore known by what was formerly called in England an eke (i.e. added) name.

It later became *nekename* and slovenly pronunciation eventually turned this into nickname. The renowned Dr Johnson thought the word derived from the French *nique* which means a gesture (but not a name) of mockery.

Nicknames (*llysenwau* in Welsh) are given all over Britain and were especially common in mining communities, particularly in the North East, but perhaps the most original are to be found in Wales – as can be seen later – and they seem to be in greater profusion. They are given much more spontaneously, either after a chance remark or some incident.

In Wales nicknames almost certainly began as a means of distinguishing between the thousands of Joneses, Williamses, Evanses and Robertses.

Many years ago, when there were coalmines galore in

Wales, they used to observe the tradition in the pits called The Spell. This was the time when the miners, on reaching the shaft bottom at the start of a shift, would sit in a circle swapping yarns and chatting before starting work. It was also the custom for nicknames to be allocated during The Spell.

A similar situation existed in the cabins of the slate quarries in north Wales during rest breaks.

Nicknames fall into various categories – occupations, sayings, disfigurements, houses, farms, collieries or areas; after a mother, wife or employer; big families, but mainly after some peculiarity or incident.

They are given in all walks of life – royalty, politics, the theatre, business and commerce and the church.

It is seldom, if ever, that people are called by their nicknames to their faces, schooldays possibly excepted. This is particularly the case with people with disfigurements.

So attached does a nickname become, that one often has to read the obituary notices in local newspapers to know the real name of a person! As one man told me: "Many a person's real name is used in only two places – Somerset House and the eternal one."

Typical of this was the obituary notice in a Flintshire newspaper which read: "Jones Edward Bevan (Ned Over The Wall)…" What the origin of this nickname was, I never found out, but his family on Deeside, north Wales, obviously wanted everyone to know that Ned Over The Wall had died.

In my researches, there have been many instances where no-one could recall the real name of a person who was better known by his nickname. My favourite example of this comes from Aberystwyth. In the days of the old workhouses, a man known as Wil Nell, after his mother (Wil, son of Nell) used to arrange concerts for the inmates every Sunday afternoon in the summer.

On one such occasion, the Aberystwyth British Legion Silver Band gave a concert and at the end Wil Nell gave his profound vote of thanks. In reply, the band secretary, Wally Wintle, who had recently made his home in the town, opened his remarks by saying; "I would like to thank Mr Nell…" (I can vouch for that because I was in the band that day). Few people knew that Wil's real name was William Jenkins.

All the nicknames in this book come from authentic sources and where possible I have named the villages and towns where people live. Some origins I have left vague to save embarrassment to people still living, to their relatives, or to the relatives of those who have died. In no way has this book been written to make fun of people.

Les Chamberlain
February 2013

OCCUPATIONS

Williams the Milk, Davies the Bread, Jones the Grocer. These are the kind of nicknames that are most familiar in books and films about Wales. But these are extremely unimaginative compared with many of the spontaneous and original ones given.

I am often asked how I first started collecting nicknames. It was many years ago when my wife and I were staying with her grandmother in the little village of Tanygrisiau, near Blaenau Ffestiniog.

In those days, radio reception in that area was poor and the only way people living on the coastal side of the Snowdon range could receive good reception was by having it piped over the mountains by a company specialising in that kind of work.

The cost to each household was the old one shilling and ninepence, so when the man first came to collect the weekly rental, he was immediately christened Dick One and Nine.

Morbid though it might seem, undertakers are the recipients of nicknames. One in west Wales was known as Evans the Death, while another in the Machynlleth area, Percy Edwards, was known as Perce the Hearse. A less reverent name was given to an undertaker in Merthyr Tydfil who was known as John the Planter. In a similar vein, an insurance agent in the Rhondda Valley was known as Dai Death Club.

In the 1930s and 1940s people used to sell wet fish from barrows, going from house to house and in Blaenau Ffestiniog there was Jack Jones the Fish and another called Wmffra 'Sgodyn Mawr (Big Fish Humphrey).

Albert Davies the Fish owned a wet fish shop in Aberystwyth, but his brother was known as Evan James Belle Isle – Evan James being his Christian names and he owned a small fishing boat called The Belle Isle.

Publicans are, in many cases, known by their pubs – Frank Commercial, Thomas Nag's Head and Joe Salmon Cross Foxes. It is interesting to note that, as in all cases, there is no set pattern in the formation of nicknames. The first uses the Christian name and the pub; the second, the surname and the pub and the third uses all three.

Other pub examples are Eric Blue Bell, Jennie Griffin Inn, Emrys the Bull (Bull's Head), Harold and Joe Grapes, Len Coach (Coach and Horses), and Tommy Queen's (Queen's Head).

Many of these names are still used, though the pubs have long since been demolished or the named persons have retired or left the licensed trade.

People's trades are a natural for nicknames. An extremely original one comes from Llangollen, Denbighshire, where a milkman with blond hair was known as Harry Gold Top. Another clever one came from south Wales where a man nicknamed Dai Narod worked for the Dynarod company.

Equally subtle was the one given to a man from Blaenau Ffestiniog. He was called Jack Codi Baw (Jack Pick Up Dirt) because he drove a JCB – the initials of his Welsh nickname.

You would think that the name Bill the Dole was given to someone who claimed unemployment benefit regularly, but not so. He was in fact Bill Edwards who lived in Wrexham and paid out dole money each week.

Tom Evans, the manager of a tyre distributors in Aberystwyth, was known to everyone as Tommy Tyres, while a man who worked on a gang erecting poles for the Merseyside and North Wales Electricity Board in Gwynedd, was known as Robin Polion (Robin the Poles). Dick Stop and Go was the name given to a north Wales man whose job it was to repair traffic lights.

A gruesome nickname comes from Bangor, north Wales. In the old C&A Hospital, now demolished, a surgeon was known as Owen Llaw Goch (Red Hand Owen) while an anaesthetist there was known as Jones the Gas and an orthopaedic surgeon as Jones the Bones.

People living near a canal often refer to it as The Cut – especially in the Midlands. Bill the Cut, however, lived in Froncysyllte near Llangollen, and worked on the Shropshire Union Canal there.

Nicknames are no respecters of persons. There was a bank manager in north Wales named Owen, but known as Owin' the Bank, a pun on owing the bank money.

The railways were another source of nicknames. An engine driver from Colwyn Bay was known as Dai Loco while others were always referred to as John Jones Driver, Tom Porter and Jones Platelayer.

In Aberystwyth, Jack Davies was one of the engine drivers on the narrow-gauge Vale of Rheidol Railway which runs to the tourist attraction at Devil's Bridge. He was known

Dai Loco

as Jack Lein Fach (Jack Little Line). The railway has always been known to locals as the Lein Fach.

Wil Keeper could easily have been a railway crossing keeper or even a footballer, but in fact he was a gamekeeper on an estate near Blaenau Ffestiniog.

The same nickname can stem from two different situations. Dai the Goat, who used to keep goats, was a former town crier in Haverfordwest, Pembrokeshire, while Ned the Goat was a soldier who used to be the goat sergeant leading the mascot of the Royal Welch Fusiliers in front of ceremonial parades.

Another example is Jones the Cop and Ianto Copper. The former was the manager of the Co-operative store (such names could be found in towns in many parts of Wales) and the latter was a policeman stationed in Aberystwyth.

The police force is another goldmine for nicknames. A policeman in the Rhyl area was known simply as Ho-ho because whenever he caught anyone up to mischief he would say: "Ho-ho, what are you up to?"

In Colwyn Bay, the headquarters of North Wales Police, Chief Superintendent John Bunting was known to all as Jack Flags, while another officer stationed in Wrexham was known to everyone as Jack Spangles because he was always eating sweets of that name. Trevor Steel Chest was also a Wrexham bobby and in the nearby village of Rhosllanerchrugog, there was a policeman called Pussyfoot because of the way he crept up on suspects.

Still in Rhos, as it is known locally, Pint of Lager was the name given to an Inspector who, while on duty, used to nip into the Grapes public house for a crafty drink.

When there was a fully-manned police station in Llangollen some years ago, there was a crop of nicknamed policemen. There was The Olympic Torch because having an office job he never went out and The Moth, allegedly because he did not like the dark and kept to street lights.

Goldfinger was a very heavy smoker and had nicotine stains on a finger while The Dalek wore an overcoat which almost touched the ground.

Still in Wrexham, a police officer, D.R. Jones, was known to his colleagues as The Doc because of his initials, but in south Wales a doctor was affectionately known to his patients as Dai Doctor.

Work akin to a policeman's is that of a prison warder and one in Cardiff Jail was known as Hugh Pugh the Screw.

Journalists are often the recipients of nicknames. Kelvin MacKenzie, the one-time controversial editor of *The Sun,* was known to his admirers as Magnificent Mac, while to his critics he was The Tabloid Terror.

Andrew Neil, a former editor of *The Sunday Times,* later to have his own shows on television, was known to his staff as Brillo because his hairstyle resembled a Brillo pad.

In the *Wrexham Leader* office in bygone days, nearly every journalist had a nickname. Ron the Butts was Ron Challoner, who was given the name in his young days because he took a quantity of sandwiches to work with him and ate them throughout the day. For the uninitiated, butts is short for butties, which is the common term for sandwiches in Wales.

In the same era was Gwyn Jones y Cardiau (Gwyn Jones the Cards) who was proficient at card tricks and Bill Rogers, named the Clagger, because he always used the forces' slang saying: "I'm in the clag" meaning he was in trouble. The Loppington Terror was a trainee reporter who was a bit of a tearaway and originated from the Shropshire village of Loppington, while The Spartan was a pseudonym used by soccer writer Gwyn Hughes.

Most of the sports writers in those days had pseudonyms. When I worked on the *Coventry Evening Telegraph,* the soccer writer always reported under the name of Nemo while the rugby reporter was Nimrod.

At one time sports reporters could choose their own pen names. One named John Cotton in Wrexham chose Job, after the Biblical character. Asked why he had chosen that name, he replied that it was all right for the other writers to have names like The Spartan because they covered the big games, but it needed the patience of Job to cover games like Penycae v Brymbo, two village teams.

Still with newspapers, there were three circulating at one time in the Blaenau Ffestiniog area – *Y Rhedegydd, Y Glorian* and *Y Gloch*. The correspondents for each were known as Davies Rhedegydd (William Davies), Now Glorian (Owen Hughes – Now being a Welsh contraction for Owen) and Lewis Gloch (Lewis Davies).

In Aberystwyth, a reporter on the now defunct *Welsh Gazette* was known to everyone as Parry Gazette, while a colleague was always referred to as Tommy Ginger because he had red hair.

I am often asked if nicknames are still given today and the reply is yes, but possibly not in such profusion. On one of my previous newspapers, one of the women in the advertising department was known as Road Runner after the bird cartoon character, because she always rushed about with her high heels clacking. She was also called Raffles because whenever there was a raffle, it was she who went round with the tickets.

Another employee was given two nicknames. The first was Herr Flick because he vaguely resembled the head of the Gestapo in the television series *'Allo 'Allo*. Later he was christened Lord Lucan because, so the story goes, there had been a delay in getting the newspaper printed and heads of department held an inquest as to why it had happened. When the gentleman in question arrived halfway through the meeting, the chairman is alleged to have said: "Ah, here comes Lord Lucan." Asked why he had been called that, the reply was: "Whenever there is trouble, you disappear!"

There was a brilliant artist on the newspaper named Michael Roberts whom I christened Michaelangelo, while a computer operator with a beard was called Rasputin.

The company decided to bring in a young woman consultant for the sake of greater efficiency. In her first meeting she was there with her flip chart and felt-tip pen and was immediately named Miss Flip Chart.

There were three sub-editors on the newspaper with the same Christian name. Trevor Smith was called The Rev Trev because he was an ordained minister of religion, Trevor Hughes was Clever Trev because he wore glasses with thick black frames and always wore a dickie bow which made him look erudite and the third one, Trefor Williams, was Effing Trev… because he spelt his name with an f and not a v!

Another member of staff who had a deep voice and a beard was nicknamed The Troglodite and the chief feature writer, the late Tony Challis, was called Poison Chalice. I also gave him another name. He always turned up for work smartly dressed, but one afternoon he came into the office dressed in muddy jeans, boots and an old anorak. A great walker, he had been over the hills with his dog on his day off and had called in the office to pick up some work. As soon as he appeared, I shouted out: "Why, it's Baldrick" after the character in the television series *Black Adder*, and the name stuck.

A great character in Wrexham known by almost everybody is photographer Les Evans who worked on the *Evening Leader* but is now a freelance. Someone gave him the name Toulouse-Lautrec because he is so short and has a beard. He was a good one for giving nicknames.

Two nicknames were given to a young trainee journalist on the same paper. The first was Osram, because he had a bald head resembling the electric light bulb made by that firm, and the second was Meat and Two Veg because he always went home for his lunch while other reporters ate in the canteen or at their desks.

Andrew Forgrave, who became an outstanding feature writer on the *Daily Post,* was given the name The Colonel because of his military bearing and cut-glass accent compared with the other youngsters, and possibly because his late father had been a Lieutenant Colonel in the army. Another trainee was christened Space Cadet, because she always seemed to be in another world.

In Welshpool a reporter was known as Idwal Live and Dead because he had written so many wedding reports and obituaries. Again in the newspaper industry, a printer in Llangefni, Anglesey, was known as Dai Indian Ink.

The coal mines, as indicated earlier, were always a good source for nicknames. Twm y Dogi was the name given to a platelayer underground in south Wales, but I have failed to find the origin of the name.

In the days of wooden supports and props, sawn off-cuts would be taken home for fire wood, so miners were given names such as John Block and Sammy Sticks.

All the pit ponies had names and the men who led them

usually had those names added after their own, as in Huw Champion and John Boxer.

An under manager at one pit was known as Ifans y Gaffer (Evans the Boss), while Reuben y Fittar was of course a fitter and Jack y Brici was a bricklayer.

Huw Bevin sounds a legitimate name for a person, but it was the name given to one of the first Bevin Boys to work at the Point of Ayr Colliery near Prestatyn. Bevin Boys were young men who, instead of being called up for the forces during the Second World War, were conscripted to work down coalmines. It was a scheme introduced by Government minister Ernest Bevin.

Emlyn Lamp Room, as the name suggests, worked in the lamp room of a north Wales pit where the lamps for the miners' helmets were kept, while Bill Lamps did the same work in a south Wales pit.

Ned the Lighthouse seems an odd name for a coalminer, but it was the name given to a miner who lived near the Point of Ayr lighthouse. Another Ned was Ned Trowsus Gwyn (White Trousers Ned). Many years ago miners wore white trousers made of calico to reflect what little light came from their lamps and Ned was the last miner to wear such trousers at the Point of Ayr Colliery.

There was a great deal of mischief in the giving of nicknames. A typical example was Twm Coler (Tom the Collar). He was a very naive man whose first job was that of a miner. Later he became a fireman at the pit. Miners never wore a collar and tie at work, so when Tom was given his new job, his boss teased him that now he had been promoted he would have to turn up in a collar and tie. On his first day as a fireman, sure enough Tommy turned up in a clean collar and tie, much to the amusement of his workmates because firemen did not wear a collar and tie either.

A sad story lies behind the name Wil Griffiths y Te (Will Griffiths the Tea). After the General Strike of 1926, miners had to 'crawl' back in humiliating circumstances begging for work. Day after day they were told by the bosses: "No work today, come back tomorrow." This went on for a number of years. Will was one of the last to be reinstated and in the years he was away from the pit, he eked out a meagre living going from door to door in the area selling packets of tea from a suitcase. All the miners' families bought tea from him and that is how he came by his name.

A man who worked on the furnaces at Point of Ayr was known as Twll Tân (Fire Hole) and a surface worker was called Sei'r Iard Lo (Isaiah the Coal Yard).

Bob the Garth was known by the name of the village where he lived. When he too became a fireman, part of his work involved testing for gas underground so he then became known as Bob the Gas instead.

Two Foot Jones might sound like a dwarf, but in fact he was a south Wales miner who was used to working in a coal seam only two feet high. Jack the Paint was the miners' affectionate name for Jack Crabtree, the first artist ever to go on the National Coal Board's payroll. As the official artist, he was given a free rein to join miners on their shifts in collieries near his home in Newport, Gwent.

Some unpleasant names are given in certain circumstances. A man who was in charge of the sewerage works in a south Cardiganshire town had the unfortunate name of Tom Cachu, this being the Welsh swear word for excreta.

A Mr Harse moved to Wales from England and was immediately given the name Dai Bum. Another was very proud that he had never been given a nickname in a north Wales village where nickname-giving was prevalent. It was his daughter's wedding, however, that earned him his name. When the wedding report appeared in the local newspaper, one part read: "…and the bride carried a bouquet of shite freesias." The misprint meant that her father was forever called Davies Shite.

Although times change, nicknames stick, as in the case of a garage owner in the Snowdonia village of Bethesda. He was known as Harri Bach Chwech a Dime (Little Harry Sixpence Ha'penny). He was a diminutive man who used to run charabanc trips before the war, costing each passenger the old sixpence halfpenny, but the name stuck long after he raised the price.

Sometimes, as in the name Twll Tân above, the nickname does not contain the person's Christian or surname. Another example is High Trucks, a tinplate worker from Britton Ferry, Carmarthenshire. His name was Bryn Richards and his job was to drive a truck that carried the long sheets of tinplate. Few people in the factory knew his real name.

Williams y Bont (Williams the Bridge) was a butcher whose shop, now demolished, stood at the end of Trefechan Bridge, Aberystwyth. Nicknames were not always given to avoid confusion between two people with the same name or trade, but Llew Rowlands the Butcher was always known to everybody in Aberystwyth by that name, although there was no confusion involved.

Clergy are also fair game for nicknames. The late Roman Catholic Archbishop of Liverpool, the Most Reverend Derek Warlock and the former Bishop of Liverpool, the Right Reverend David Sheppard, worked together for 20 years putting aside their religious differences to help Liverpool through the Militant crisis, the Toxteth riots and the Heysel and Hillsborough football disasters. They were sometimes known as the Mersey Miracle, the Dynamic Duo and Fish and Chips – the last because they always appeared together in newspapers!

A vicar in a north Wales town was known as The Mikado after the way he held up both arms at one stage of the service. The person who gave him that name said it always reminded him of the entrance of the Mikado in the Gilbert and Sullivan opera when he sang: "My object all sublime I shall achieve in time…"

Many years ago in Rhosllanerchrugog, officials were interviewing candidates for the post of minister at their chapel. One minister told the deacons of his vast theological works and mentioned a number of degrees that could be put after his name. He then said: "But I want to be called the Reverend, pure and simple." He was appointed minister, but from then on was known to everyone as the Reverend Pure and Simple.

Many churches and chapels in Wales rely on lay preachers who travel round a vast area preaching in different places of worship. One such man was known as Jones Pregeth

Mawr (Big Sermon Jones) because he was noted for his long sermons. In a similar vein, a minister in a chapel in Llandudno Junction was given the name Pregeth Chwarter Awr (the Quarter-of-an-Hour Sermon) because his sermons always lasted 15 minutes.

The Set Fawr (Big Seat) in chapels is an area in front of the pulpit where the deacons – church elders – sit. To be made a deacon in the old days was indeed an honour and when it happened to a man in a north Wales village, he proudly told everyone about it and was immediately called Dic Set Fawr (Big Seat Dick).

Here is a miscellany of nicknames from occupations. Willie Jarvis opened a bingo hall in Wrexham and was straight away called Willie Bingo. A tailor in Llanelli was known as Dai Ready-Made, and Jones the Stitch was a tailor who lived in Denbighshire.

An architect on Anglesey was named Dic ARIBA because of his qualification letters after his name. Dic Bach Prynhawn (Little Dick Afternoon), who always worked the afternoon shift at his factory, lived in Machynlleth, Powys, and Dai Rats was the rodent officer in Rhos. Derek Two Boats lived in Rhyl where he owned two boats!

Wil Casgen Gwrw (Beer Barrel Will) was a man who rolled the barrel of ale to thirsty workers in a south Wales factory. Bill the Bladder Blower was reputed to be the last sausage maker in Aberystwyth. He was William Shurrin who worked for H.P. Edwards, butchers, and had to blow up the pig's bladder to obtain dripping.

In Buckley, Flintshire, a shoe repairer was known as Dick Gutta Percha because he used that substance to repair shoes. Another shoe repairer in the town was called Billy the Nailer.

Dai Rowlands y Clochydd (Dai Rowlands the Bell Ringer) was a sexton in St Mary's Church, Aberystwyth, and in the same town was Tommy Gas, a gas inspector. Eric the Click was a photographer in Kenfig Hill, south Wales, while Eddie Click Click was a photographer in Carmarthenshire.

Jones the Yeast was a representative for a yeast firm in mid Wales and supplied the bakery of Glyn James y Bara (Glyn James the Bread) among others, in Aberystwyth.

Don Witness Box was a solicitor's son in the Abergele area and Arthur Whitewash was a painter and decorator. Mr Tic Toc was a clock and watch repairer in Wrexham and an Abergele man in the same trade was known as Dick Clocks and Dick Tic Toc.

An obituary notice in a north Wales newspaper announced that Tadeusz Robinson had died, but after his name was his nickname in brackets, Ted Antiques.

Nicknames in this category could fill many pages, but that should give readers a good idea of how nicknames develop from occupations and professions.

DISFIGUREMENTS

It may seem cruel to many that people with disfigurements are given nicknames, but they are not given with the intention of poking fun but again merely to differentiate between people with similar names. In some cases they are given as a form of affection.

Subtlety comes to the fore in these nicknames as in many others, and a good example is that of Owen Nine Months who lived in Tonypandy. The lobe of one of his ears was shot off in the First World War and this left him with three quarters of a (y)ear. In Llanelli lived Dai Eighteen Months because he had a whole ear and a half of one, while a man from north Wales with only one ear was known as Bob Un Glust (Bob One Ear).

Another First World War victim was known – but certainly not to his face – as Georgie One Ball because it was alleged he had lost a testicle after being wounded.

The old proboscis is often a target for a nickname such as Bill Parrot and Hugh Hook Nose. Similarly Wally Bent Axle received the name because of his crooked nose.

And the eyes have it too with such names as Teddy Cock-Eye and Will Cockle Eye, both of whom had squints. Then of course, there was Johnny One Eye and Tommy Nelson.

Dai Up and Down walked with a limp as did Tom Dot and Carry One, a Welshman living in Solihull who had a wooden leg. Tom Nothing Straight had a disfigured arm and leg and a bent nose.

One of the nicknames I am always being told of is Dai Central Eating. Whether so many were genuine I know not, but it is a name I gave to a friend of mine, Barrie Clark, when we worked together in Coventry. He had just one tooth sticking up in the bottom of his mouth, so I christened him Barrie Central Eating.

John Pen Mawr (John Big Head) was not given the name because of his boasting and arrogance but because he literally had a very large head for the size of his body, while Wil Llais Main (Will Thin Voice) and Wil Sgrech (Will Scream) had very high-pitched voices.

Tommy Titanic weighed 20 stones while Little Johnny One Inch was a very short man as was Twt Ellis, twt being a Welsh word for tiny. Poker Berry was so-named because he walked as erect as the smartest guardsman, likewise Will Straight Back.

Dai Cnau means Dai Nuts and like John Cwcw (John Cuckoo) the name was given to men who were a little bit simple. George y Frest (George the Chest) was always short of breath because he suffered from a bad chest, as was the case of John Dim Gwynt (John No Wind).

Dai Deaf, again as the name suggests, was stone deaf and was a handyman in a snooker hall in Aberystwyth. A hirsute man from Rhosllanerchrugog was known as Ned y Blew (Ned the Hair) and a left-handed man in the village was known as Wil Llaw Chwith (Left Hand Will). There was a left-handed man in the town of Ruthin, Denbighshire, too, who was known as Dai Llaw Chwith.

Dai Central Eating

In south Wales a man with a humpback was known as Harry Camel and another with a similar disfigurement on Anglesey was called Wil Tatws (Will Potatoes) because his hump gave the impression that he was carrying a sack of potatoes on his back.

The One-Arm Bandit was the name given to a teacher in Wigan because he had only one arm, while Dai Sloping lived in Ruabon, near Wrexham, and was given the name because he had one leg shorter than the other. He was a good cricketer and when bowling nearly always bowled an unplayable shot.

In south Wales a man who had one arm shorter than the other was known as Tommy Clock and a man in mid Wales with a similar disfigurement was called Harry Half Past Five.

NAMES AFTER TOWNS, COLLIERIES, STREETS ETC.

Whenever a man moved to work in a new area, he invariably had the name of the town or area where he had come from appended to his name.

An Englishman moving to a Welsh community usually had 'y Sais' added, as in Jac y Sais (Jack the Englishman). But at Point of Ayr a man called Wil y Sais had been born and bred in Wales and one can only assume that his father or grandfather had been given the name on moving from England and that the name had been passed on as is often the case from father to son.

John Llaneg – short for Llanegryn, near Tywyn in Gwynedd, was the name given to John Evans by the Welsh community in Wolverhampton when he moved there. Other examples are Dafydd Llanrwst (Dafydd being the Welsh for David), Bill Birkenhead who lived in Llangollen but whose family originated from the Mersey town, Martha Harlech, Ben Bala, John Caernarfon, William Jones Bagillt, John Williams Point (of Ayr) and Lei (Elias) Denbigh.

Miners were often named after the collieries where they worked, as in the case of Evans Deep Dyffryn and Twm Llai Men (Tom Llay Main), while others were named after the street where they lived as in Charlie Jones Queen, Wil Tŷ Crwn (Will Round House) who lived in a house of that description and John Ceg Twnnel (John Tunnel Mouth) who lived near the entrance to a railway tunnel.

In Denbighshire there was a farm called White House Farm and one of the sons who lived there was called Perce White House, while not far away at Brown Cow Farm, one of the sons was nicknamed Will Brown Cow.

Examples of being named after houses include Jo Hen Stabl (Joe Old Stable), Bob Tan y Capel (Bob Below the Chapel), and Jones Hafod (Jones Summer Dwelling). Names were also given after the part of a street where a person lived, such as Twm Tŷ Canol (Tom Middle House), Jim Far End, Bob Top House, John Tŷ Newydd (John New House) and Maggie Top y Rhos who lived at the top end of the village.

John Ceg Twnnel

Bob yr Hyts (Bob the Huts) was so-called because he lived in a house that had been converted from a hut that workmen had lived in when building the railway at Ffynnongroyw, Flintshire.

Perhaps the majority of people in Wales are nicknamed after the house where they live or used to live. There are numerous 'common ones' such as Robin Wern, Jack London House, Twm Ael-y-Bryn, Mrs Jones Jutland and Tommy Mefking, a Welsh corruption of Mafeking.

But one of the most intriguing stories comes from the tiny village of Llanegryn, near Tywyn, where I met the late Sam Waterloo and his wife Jennie Waterloo. The origin of this nickname dates back to the Battle of Waterloo when a young soldier from the village was reported killed in the battle. His wife refused to believe this and eventually made her way to the battlefield – no mean feat in those days. In a farm nearby, she found her husband being cared for by a

Sam Waterloo

French family and eventually brought him back to Wales. They named their little cottage Waterloo and ever since those who have lived in the cottage have had the name Waterloo tagged on to their Christian names.

CONFUSION

Nicknames are often used to avoid confusion between people of the same name. In Aberystwyth there were two men named Tommy Jones. One was known as Tommy Gee Gee because his father was a haulage contractor and, as a boy, Tommy sometimes led the horses back to the stable at night.

The other was known as Tommy Swan after the restaurant named The Swan, owned by his mother. He was also an excellent footballer who played for Aberystwyth Town and was known in that capacity as Tommy Twelver, but why I have never been able to discover.

Thomas Thomas from south Wales was known as Tom Twice and in Aberdare a schoolmaster named David Davies was called Dai Cube. William Williams was a schoolmaster in Tywyn and because there were two teachers named Williams, he became Billy Two.

THE WELSH 'ABROAD'

There is many a person walking about in England who, without knowing it, has been nicknamed by some Welsh exile.

A woman from Blaenau Ffestiniog who went to live in Wolverhampton called her corner shopkeeper Brewer Potel Saws (Brewer the Sauce Bottle) because she said he had square shoulders like an HP Sauce bottle. She also christened a neighbour Mr Davies yr Arch (Mr Davies the Coffin) because he had a flowerbed in his front garden in the shape of a coffin.

Bill Bennett was the classified advertising manager on the *Coventry Evening Telegraph* where I once worked. We were both rugby fanatics and used to have a 10p bet on international games – he always took England or whichever country was playing against Wales while naturally I backed Wales or whichever country was playing England. One day the news desk secretary, Val Underhill, who had lived in Wales and knew the habit of giving nicknames, said to me: "Billy 10p wants you to phone him." From then on he was known to everyone as Billy 10p!

FOREIGN NICKNAMES

People of other nationalities give nicknames in similar fashion.

While in Honfleur, France, I came across a man whose nickname was Sous-marin (Submarine). Apparently he was a well-known local drunk and when being chased by police he would dive into the old harbour there to avoid being arrested. He then claimed that only the naval police could catch him!

Champêtre was a name given to a country bumpkin, while La Fanfare (the band) was the name given to someone with a loud voice. Nez Plat was a man with a flat nose and Nez de Pioche had a hook nose. Le Petit Tambour was a little drummer in a band and Gros Bouton meant Big Pimple.

In Germany I came across a young man named Volker Lübke who was called The Professor because of the style of glasses he wore and a teacher called Glatze (No Hair) because he was bald.

In the Pacific island of Papua New Guinea, once part of the British Empire, Queen Elizabeth was known endearingly as Big Fellah Mama Kwin while Prince Philip had the delightful name of Man Belong Mama Kwin. Prince Charles, Prince of Wales, was called Pikinini Belong Big Fellah Mama Kwin.

DUPLICATE NAMES

Although earlier in this book I wrote that most nicknames stay for life, there are a few exceptions. Some people have been given two, or even three different names during their lifetime.

Bill 'Portmadoc' Jones of Rhosllanerchrugog was typical. As a youngster living in his hometown of Porthmadog, Gwynedd, he was called Cochyn (Redhead) because of his ginger hair. He moved to Rhos to work in the nearby Bersham Colliery and was immediately given the name Bill Portmadoc. But whenever he visited his home town after that, he was referred to as Bill Rhos – the wheel had turned full circle.

The only other triple nickname I have come across belonged to a William Evans. As a young man in Blaenau Ffestiniog, he was known as Wil Eve which is short for Evans, but when he moved to Porthmadog he took up watch and clock repairing as a hobby and became renowned for his work renovating grandfather clocks, so he then became known as Wil Clociau (Will the Clocks). On retirement, he moved to Dolgellau and lived in a house called Waterloo and became known there as Wil Waterloo.

Perhaps two of the most amusing in this category come from Swansea and Radnorshire. The Swansea one refers to the wife of an egg supplier who was known as Dai Eggs. She became Mrs Dai Eggs, but from the day she gave birth to twins, she became known as Mrs Dai Double Yolk.

The other example refers to an employee at the Elan Valley reservoirs. He was known as Idwal Crust because he nearly always had a crust in his lunchbox. Princess Margaret came there on a royal visit and shook hands with him. From then on he was known as Idwal Upper Crust!

SCHOOLDAYS

No doubt we can all give hundreds of examples of nicknames when we were at school. They provide the greatest number, but they do not necessarily stick afterwards. Both staff and pupils are victims and here are some of my recollections from Ardwyn Grammar School in Aberystwyth.

My headmaster, D.C. Lewis, was known as Dai Bol (Dai Stomach) for obvious reasons, while his son was called Colin Chest, because someone said he had a pigeon chest. One of the music teachers was called Wil Cab, short for Wil Cabbage, because of his crinkly hair which someone, probably a pupil, thought resembled a cabbage after it had been shredded. His son was known as Sprouts.

A master with a double chin was obviously called Chin and others included Cy Snake, Lewis the Nark and Puff and Blow. The latter was also known as Piggy Bach (Little Pig), because a mischievous pupil thought his face resembled that of a piglet.

Latin teacher Miss Irene Davies was known as Davws Latin, while Dr Ethel Jones, the Senior Mistress and Head of French, was affectionately known to all simply as Doc.

And now the nicknames of some of the pupils. Winwns (Welsh for onions) was a corruption of his name Wyn Hughes, while his best friend Reg Salmon was called Sammy by everyone. Arab was a tall, dark-skinned lad and

Garage lived in a nearby village where his father owned a garage. Titch was obviously on the short side and another diminutive lad was called The Flea. Willy Bumps, who became an eminent surgeon, had a large lump on his temple.

Joe Black had very black eyebrows and Bush had a mass of tight curls. His is one name that stuck because he became secretary of the old pupils' Ardwynian Association and was still known as Bush until his death, even signing his letters to members as Bush.

Dai Fat was a very rotund lad, as was Jumbo, while Cochyn was a redhead. Cacen (Welsh for cake) lived in a café and a very good friend of mine was called Winks, a shortened form of his surname, Wintle. He was the son of the secretary of the Aberystwyth British Legion Band mentioned earlier.

Ronnie Hutchings Jones was always known as Hutch, and Ponky was a pupil who played the tenor drum in the army cadet band.

Although the origin of the above is obvious, no-one has been able to shed light on any of the following: Wuckie (to rhyme with lucky), Bullet, Pan, Bum, Twala, Taxi, Jeep, Spud, Bandy, Simple (he was actually a very clever pupil who became an accountant), Barney (who became Chief Executive of a health authority in south Wales), Pudding, Twten (potato), Popeye, Biff (who went on to play for Arsenal), Botchy, Wiwa, Flash, Sunshine, John Buddah, Texas, Wiggy, Jasper, and Ronux.

There were three brothers called Gogo Mawr (Big Gogo, the eldest), Gogo Canol (Middle Gogo) and Gogo Bach

(Little Gogo, the youngest). The only girls I can remember having nicknames were Squeaks (also the name given to her brother), and Pinky.

WOMEN

Compared with men, very few women have been given nicknames as far as I have been able to ascertain. Certainly women with nicknames are in the minority.

They too fall into the familiar categories. In the occupation section we have Big Maud the Fish, a rather large woman as the name suggests, who sold wet fish off a barrow in Aberystwyth, Harriet Tŷ Popty (Harriet the Bakery) in south Wales, and Mary Parlwrs who lived in Llangollen and was given the name before the last war when only front parlours of houses were papered and she used to do paper-hanging as a spare-time job.

In the characteristics category we have Hanna Fechan (Little Hannah) and Mary Pen Wen (White Haired Mary). Mary Pakistan one night went to the harbour of a seaside town and dropped big stones on to a fishing boat because she thought it was being used to bring illegal immigrants into the country. In my home town we had two characters called Happy Agnes and Kitty Pontin, but we never knew their real names.

In the houses category I well remember Mrs Jones Jutland who had a relative who had fought in the famous battle of Jutland. My mother's best friend, known as Maggie Pen, short for Margaret Penelope, was the wife of Jack Lein Fach mentioned earlier.

In the peculiarities class we have Lisi Tebot (Lizzie

Teapot), a prolific tea-drinker, and Maggie Hughes Catalogue who was an agent for a mail order firm. Mrs Jones Pay Cash abhorred hire purchase and always started a transaction by saying: "I will be paying in cash."

Alice Royal Mail, whose uncle was one of the first postmen in the town to push the wicker-type basket truck with Royal Mail written on the side, lived in Blaenau Ffestiniog. During the school holidays she always walked with him on his deliveries.

Mrs Jones Unig (Lonely Mrs Jones) was the name given to a north Wales widow while Jenny Quack Quack lived in a village near Prestatyn and was said to have kept ducks in her house. In the same village, Mrs Jones South Africa was so-named because her son emigrated to that country.

Less complimentary names include Mary Slei (Sly Mary) and Maggie News of the World, a village gossip. A woman in another north Wales village spoke very quickly and used to get very annoyed when the lads of the village played football on ground next to her home. She would chase them, at the same time shouting at a terrific speed, with the result that they named her Maggie Machine Gun.

A snobbish English woman who came to live in Wales was given the name Mrs Pen Mawr (Mrs Big Head) while Maggie Ceg Fawr (Maggie Big Mouth) was another village gossip. Then there was Mrs Williams Foghorn because she had a loud voice, and Maggie Prod who was a Swansea woman who always prodded her finger at people when talking to them. A woman in mid Wales was known as Nellie Carrier Bag because she always carried a carrier bag.

The Late Mrs Smith sounds as if someone is referring to a woman who has died, but it was the name given to a Wrexham woman who was always late for church. The same applied to Maggie Trên Naw (Maggie Nine O'Clock Train) because she always arrived late for chapel, just as the 9pm train from Llandudno to Blaenau Ffestiniog often arrived late.

A north Wales woman who lived on a farm noted for its new potatoes was known to the locals as Margaret Tatws Newydd (Margaret New Potatoes), while another who lived in St Asaph, Denbighshire, was known as The Humming Bird because she always sang or hummed at work.

When someone does something for the first time, or something happens for the first time, you can guarantee that a nickname will be forthcoming. Such was the case with Mary Bow because her house in Penrhyndeudraeth, Gwynedd, was one of the first in the village to have bow windows.

A Denbigh woman was always called Britannia after playing that part in a pageant in the town. Also there was The Giraffe, the name given to a very tall woman who rode an old-fashioned 'sit-up-and-beg' bicycle.

When Wellington bombers were pasting Nazi Germany in the Second World War, their crews thanked the magnificent workers who built those gigantic planes. One of them was Joyce Jones who lived in Hawarden, near Chester. As a 17-year-old who did not know one end of a screwdriver from another, she went to work at the then Vickers Armstrong factory in nearby Broughton. Joyce fitted the bomb aimer's window in the belly of the aircraft and it involved using black Bostick sealant. She said: "My Mum sent me to work in white overalls and on Monday I was Snow White, but by Friday they were calling me Little Miss Bostick.

A former receptionist at the Department of Social Security offices in Wrexham was given the nickname Fast Flo because of the hundreds of people she dealt with in the busy office every day.

Kath Hirst was a woman with civic pride. Every day, come rain or shine, she could be seen walking around her home town in search of abandoned shopping trolleys and returning them to the Kwik Save store. It is estimated that in four years she returned 15,000 from alleys, parks, skips and streams and as a result she became known as The Trolleybasher.

A downmarket tabloid newspaper very unkindly nicknamed Ann Widdecombe, a Home Office Minister in a previous Conservative government, Doris Karloff after the legendary Frankenstein star, Boris. This was because she sparked a national uproar over her insistence that pregnant women prisoners should be handcuffed and chained when in hospital to prevent them escaping. She was a big enough politician to laugh the name off.

IRA terrorist Donna Maguire was nicknamed the Angel of Death after being found guilty in Germany of helping to plant five huge bombs intended to kill five soldiers as they slept in their barrack block in Osnabrück.

But back to the amusing nicknames. You would have thought Nansi Overseas was given the name because she had lived abroad. But no, she was a Pwllheli woman who had at one time lived just across the water on Bardsey Island.

A teacher in Swansea was known to her pupils as Ma Bun because she wore her hair in a bun and in the same school another was known as Boogwig because she wore a wig, while Miss Williams Earphones had a bun on each side of her head.

In Ruabon, a woman who always brought out the best china when she had visitors became Mrs Bone China. Rhyming came into the name given to a telephonist working for a Wrexham firm – hence Joan the Phone, and Mrs Bacon in south Wales was known to all as Streaky.

I have come across many nicknames where the origins are unknown. Typical are: Mrs One Kipper, Sophie Tra-la-la, Laura Bo-Bo, Mrs Leather Belly, Betty Boopah, Mari Pisin Tair (Mary Threepenny Bit) and Mighty Madge.

PERSONAL TRAITS AND APPEARANCES

Many people receive nicknames as a result of their appearance or a personal trait. Few realise they have earned a nickname and would no doubt be offended if they did know.

Such was the case of Herb Muck, a scruffy-looking councillor in a north Wales town. Another councillor was known as Solid Mahogany because people thought him 'thick'.

Some discover their nickname by accident. The former City Treasurer in Coventry, Dr A.H. Marshall, was at a meeting of retired officers when the Lord Mayor, Councillor G. Sheridan, let out the secret of the name used behind his back when at work. He had the reputation of being in favour of cautious spending when he advised committees what the council could and could not afford. He was greatly amused when told his nickname was The Abominable-No Man.

A nickname acquired at school can remain with a person into adulthood even though circumstances change. A boy in a village on the A5 was known as Willie Stinkie because he came from a poor family and smelled. He eventually went to university and became a clever professional man, but to those who were in school with him he was still known as Willie Stinkie.

There was a character in the village of Penycae near Wrexham who was known as Billy Whizz because he always rode a bike at high speed. He was also known as the Mayor of Penycae.

As you may have already gathered, the village of Rhosllanerchrugog was a rare place for giving nicknames. There was the Roof Inspector so-named because he always looked up at the ceiling when talking to someone. There were two men in the village with very pale faces – one was known as John Calch (John Whitewash) and the other as Mr Ghostie. A police inspector was known locally as Pint of Lager because that was his favourite drink.

Ifan Full Pelt was always in a hurry and only had time to say hello, while Jack Storom (Jack Storm) always spoke

Pint of Lager

in a rush with a flurry of words and stuttered whenever he was excited.

Clothes are always prominent in giving nicknames. Jane Sanau (Jane Socks) always went about wearing ankle socks while Idris Clogs is self-explanatory and Phil Sgidie (Phil Shoes) worked in a shoe shop.

Tomi Crys Glan (Tommy Clean Shirt) always went to work in a clean shirt and Wil Wasgod (Wil Waistcoat) was never seen without that garment. Two others associated with clothing were Sami Rhaff (Sammy Rope) whose trousers were always kept up with a piece of string and Glyn Patch. His name came about because when he went to school in the days before the last war, he had a larger patch in his trousers than any of the other boys. Teddy Carpiau (Teddy Rags) was always scruffily dressed. Dafydd Pwrs (David Purse) would not trust his wife with the housekeeping money and always kept the household purse himself.

Some years ago I was compering a brass band and choir concert at the Central Methodist Hall, Coventry. The choir was one of the best in south Wales and the hall was full. As I was getting changed for the concert, the choir's conductor rushed into the room saying: "Have you seen Rasputin?" I did not have a clue whom he was talking about so he explained that it was the choir's accompanist. I did not see the said gentleman until I went on stage to introduce him. When I did see him with his thin, gaunt face and straggling beard, I could quite understand why he had been given that nickname. The flamboyant conductor then came on after being introduced, wearing a full-length black cape with bright red silk lining and I felt like calling him the Caped Crusader!

A Wrexham headmaster was known in his young days in Ruthin as Dai Beatly because he had a Beatles-style haircut, while at the other extreme a bald-headed man in south Wales and another in Wrexham were both called Shiny Joe. Continuing the hair theme, Ginger Tom from Swansea wore a ginger wig while Wili Bach Dandruff (Little Willy Dandruff) always had his collar covered in dandruff.

In Pontardawe, south Wales, I found a man called Dai Droopy because he always looked miserable, and in another town Billy Slow Puncture was so-named because he had a speech impediment. Dai Llwnci Swllt (Dai Swallowed a Shilling) from Denbigh spoke as if he had something stuck in his throat.

Some names are sarcastic as in Dai Good Sort who was supposed to be the meanest man in town and Jac Sebon (Jack Soap), a scruffy individual who, according to locals, hardly ever washed.

Nicknames often arise as a result of food and drink. Jones Caerphilly always ate cheese sandwiches for his lunch at work while Dai Brown Ale always drank that at his local. Jones Pop Bottle was a well-known teetotaller in his Valleys town. Dewi Dyfrwr (Dewi the Water Drinker) was another teetotaller who, in his pursuit of temperance, said he was following the example of the Patron Saint of Wales, Dewi Sant (Saint David) who reputedly drank only water.

Stan Chips was a prolific chips eater and Dai Chips owned a south Wales fish and chip shop, while Twm Bacwn (Tom Bacon) of course loved bacon. Then there were John Cabbage, Raymond Cakes, John Hovis, John Jam and Tomi Caws (Tommy Cheese). A Wrexham rugby player was known as Caws because his surname was Cheesebrough. Tommy Butty was a young footballer who after every game went into the nearest cafe for a 'butty' – a piece of bread and butter.

More examples of food nicknames include Bill Dumpling, Bob Toffee, Len Pwdin Moch (Len Black Pudding), and Bill Lightcakes who, along with his brother, inherited the name because their grandmother used to cook and sell such delicacies. A whole family in Rhos carried the label Butter and Eggs after their name because their grandparents owned a shop selling these items.

In days gone by housewives used to make their own dough for bread and take it to the local baker for baking. Hywel Toes (Hywel Dough) was so-named because his mother used to bake the bread in her bakery.

Burum is the Welsh word for yeast and Daniel Lei Burum was given the name because his grandmother used to sell it in her shop. Jim Temon used to sell tea which had the trade name Temon, and Dai Bacyn Da (Dai Good Bacon) had the name because his father had the reputation of selling good quality bacon. In north Wales, sweets are called da-da and Clifford Da-Da was so-named because his parents owned a sweet shop, but Tommy Da-Da, from a different area, was given the name because as a youngster he was always buying sweets with his pocket money.

You would think that Tom Margarine from Rhyl would fall into the food category, but not so. He acquired the name after he had repaired his front gate with a piece of wood from a margarine box.

ANIMALS

Animals also play a large part in nicknames. Twm 'Ffyle (Tom the Horses) may have been given the name for his love of horses or for betting on them! South Walian Dai Mulod (Dai Donkeys) used to own donkeys that gave rides to children at the seaside and Jack Price the Donkeys in Aberystwyth did the same. Television brought Llew the Donk his name after he was interviewed for his success in breeding a piebald donkey.

Bob Pinci Ponc could have been named after anything, but in fact he had two kittens named Pinci and Ponc, hence his nickname. Jac Bach Ffantel (Little Jack Fantail) was a little fellow whose bottom stuck out like a fantail pigeon's, while a north Wales family had Foxes after their name, some say because of their crafty nature, and Huw Llwynog (Huw the Fox) was a crafty man.

Anglesey provides Wil Milgi (Will the Greyhound) who owned a greyhound and one day it gave chase to a hare, but lost it. It is said that Will took over and caught the hare! He was a prolific walker and used to walk 10 miles each day to Llanberis and back to Anglesey. Also from the island, nicknamed the Mother of Wales, comes Jac Cwningen Wyllt (Jack the Wild Rabbit), because he was a fast runner.

Here is a miscellany of names given for various reasons. Wil 'Ard 'At was a factory worker who always wore a safety helmet, and Wil Bach Ditectif (Little Will the Detective) lived in Denbigh and was a busybody who knew everybody's business.

Windmill Wyn from Wrexham was a cricketer with an odd bowling action and, in another town, Stumper Alan was a wicketkeeper for his local team.

Dick Low Gear walked slowly and Dai Coathanger from Aberystwyth had big, square shoulders. Steven Handbag was a homosexual in south Wales, while another at the other end of the country was known as Harry the Queen.

In Llandudno, a man who had a Japanese look about him was named Tojo and, in the same town, a man who always had a scarf around his head like an Indian in cowboy films was known as Tonto.

Even a temporary incident can earn you a nickname, as in the case of Dai Silent in Ruthin who lost his voice for a short time. Clicker Bill lived in Pembrokeshire and was so-called because his false teeth were loose and clacked when he spoke.

Bob Bol Uwd (Bob Porridge Stomach) was so-named because, according to locals, he had a big stomach through eating too much porridge. Hugh Rubber Lips from north Wales had big lips and Maurice Top Note was an excellent tenor in the Froncysyllte Male Voice Choir, near Wrexham.

A tramp who was known as Tea Cosy Pete in Swansea because of his headgear, hit the headlines some years ago when he returned a wallet containing £500 to the builder who had lost it. No one knew his real name, but apparently he spent a year at university before dropping out when he and his mother were evicted from their council house. He was about 20 when he started life on the road.

In Bargoed, Glamorgan, there was a man called Tommy Blank, because, when playing dominoes at his local, he nearly always held the double blank. Billy Dagger received his name as a boy because he was always jumping on boys' backs pretending to stab them.

Ivor the Bounce was Ivor Hutchinson, an ex-boxer who was hired to stop fights on a North Sea ship used to accommodate men working on oil rigs.

They say in Wales there is only one thing worse than a snob and that's a Welsh snob, for the one thing most Welsh people can't stand is snobbishness. Any sign of it in a community and the nicknames start flying.

Thus we have: Mary Snob, Annie Aristocrat, Danny Swell in Flintshire and Ned y Swel (Ned the Swell) in Gwynedd, Mike Thomas the Squire and Nellie Stuck Up in south Wales. Before the last war Mary Tuppence always paid a penny extra to have the better seats in the cinema and Bob Matinée always went to the afternoon performances, never to the evening ones.

The head porter at the University College of Wales, Aberystwyth, was a smart, dapper man who had been a petty officer in the navy and to all the students he was known as The Admiral.

Harri Brenin (King Harry) was said to resemble the late King George VI, and Harry Governor's nickname arose because he used to drive a governor's cart.

There is a famous joke about Jones the Spy, whereby a Russian agent was parachuted into Swansea looking for a

Welshman who was spying for the Russians. He went to the street, knocked on the door and gave the password, only to be told: "Oh, it's not me you want boyo, it's Jones the Spy at No. 57." But in north Wales there was a man who was actually called Jones the Spy because he had a habit of peeping from behind his front room curtains at passers-by.

An Aberystwyth man was called Cocum and the nearest meaning of this word I can find is a crafty one or a person who lives on his wits. Bob Tink was said to have had relatives who were tinkers while Dai Banjo was brilliant on that instrument.

An unusual nickname was that of Jack Dochyn. Apparently, he had a speech impediment and used to call his teacher, a Miss Dawson, Miss Dochyn.

You would think that Jack Fat was a big man, but that was not the case. Many years ago he was a farmer in Johnstown, near Wrexham, and at the end of the harvest it was a tradition to have a harvest supper. He was carving meat there when one of his fellow farmers said that he did not want any fat, to which Jack replied: "All right then, I'll eat the fat," and from then on he was known as Jack Fat.

PECULIARITIES AND INCIDENTS

The majority of nicknames do not fall into any of the previous categories, but arise from some peculiarity or an incident in which a man or woman was involved.

You would expect that John the Baptist would have a religious connotaion, but far from it. He lived in the St Asaph area of north Wales and was a poacher who was often found in a river poaching salmon or trout.

Continuing the theme of names not always being what they appear to be, take Dai Quiet Wedding for example. He had little money and therefore had to get married in plimsoles – the equivalent of today's trainers. And Billy Never-Never sounds like a man who bought goods on hire purchase, but he was allegedly celibate.

An Aberystwyth man was known as Morris Cush and Ball. He was a very good snooker player who excelled at shots involving hitting the coloured ball resting against the cushion of the table at the same time as the white cue ball. Still in that Cardiganshire town, postman Dai Evans, who won the Military Medal in the First World War, was known to all as Dai MM.

It needs only one small incident to spark off a nickname, as in the case of Jones the Filth. He was a newsagent who lived on the north Wales coast and was a highly respected

John the Baptist

Dai Quiet Wedding

member of the community, a big chapel man who never swore, smoked or drank alcohol. One day, by mistake, a consignment of sexy girlie magazines was delivered to his shop along with the early-morning load of newspapers and magazines.

In a hurry to sell the newspapers to those off to work early, he quickly untied all the magazines and put them on the counter, so the story goes, without looking at them. Imagine the amusement – and shock – of those who saw them before he realised what had happened. He was totally innocent, but once the story got around, he was Jones the Filth from then on.

In the early days of the Campaign for Nuclear Disarmament, one of the first 'Ban the Bomb' demonstrators in Wales was a Scottish journalist named Bill Fletcher. He was working in Ammanford and sat in the middle of the main street, was arrested and eventually fined 10 shillings (50p) for causing an obstruction. He was immediately called Jock the Bomb. Some years later he became a colleague of mine on the *Coventry Evening Telegraph*.

The Band of Hope was a chapel movement for children in Wales and one of its main aims was to teach youngsters about the evils of drink. It started in the 1890s and the man who started it in Blaenau Ffestiniog was known as John Jones Band of Hope. Afterwards his children were known as Plant John Jones Band of Hope (plant being Welsh for children).

A Carmarthenshire farmer was given the name Bili Mochyn yn y Gwely (Billy Pig in the Bed) following a raid by Ministry of Food inspectors during the last war. An illicitly-killed pig was in the house and farmer Billy was in

Jones the Filth

Bili Mochyn yn y Gwely

bed with flu. To hide the carcase, his friends pushed the pig into bed with him. The outcome is obscure, but one story is that the doctor called just in time to 'save his bacon'.

Richard Evans was walking his chapel sweetheart home to her farm in Talsarnau, Gwynedd, many years ago when a big, black farm dog went for him. He was a burly ship's engineer and, as the dog attacked him, he gave it a hefty punch with his fist, allegedly killing it. As usual the story quickly got around and from then on he was known as Dic Ci Du (Black Dog Dick).

Butcher Tom the Bell was a Wrexham Football Club supporter who used to ring a huge handbell when he went to matches. He even took it with him behind the old Iron Curtain when Wrexham played in European Cup competitions.

One of the longest nicknames I have come across is John a Thân a Sigarét a Mwg a Matsian. Translated it is John and Fire and Cigarette and Smoke and a Match. His name was Jonathon and it was inevitable that a boy living in the heart of Wales with such an English name would be nicknamed. He started smoking and used to cadge cigarettes and matches – hence the name.

In one village school there were seven Davids in a class and each one was known as David One, David Two, David Three and so on. In the same school there was a boy named John Dau Dad (John Two Fathers) because his mother was twice-married.

Earlier I wrote about people's disfigurements, but there is only a small dividing line between disfigurements and characteristics. For example Dic Dau Fol (Dick Two Bellies), as the name suggests, was very fat, as was Edwin Bol Hwch (Edwin Sow's Belly). Gwilym Stiff walked stiffly and John Ffon Bren (John Walking Stick) was never seen without one, while Sam Chwerth was always laughing, chwerth being short for chwerthin (laughter in Welsh). Two with uncomplimentary names were Hari Oriog (Fickle Harry) and Twm Celwyddwr (Tom the Liar).

A man who worked in a furniture shop in Dolgellau, Gwynedd, was known as Willie Three Piece, and Robin Dale was given the name Daily Mail when he started secondary school. It is said that Noel Pin received his name because as a boy, he was terrified on seeing a pin.

The name of a lad in a north Wales village was Vincent Owen, but to everybody he was Rab because he was very dark-skinned. He resembled a coloured lad in a nearby village whose real name was Rab. Roy Doddle's real name was Dowell Hughes and the Dowell was corrupted to Doddle, while Sooty resembled Harry Corbett's glove puppet of that name. Teddy Bells once worked in a shop called Bell's Stores and although he left there after a short while, the name stayed with him.

Many people are known only by their initials – J.L. or T.J. A maths teacher in my school was known simply as I.T. – and others have shortened or corrupted forms of their names such as Jobat (John Robert Ellis) and Lei Gab (Elias Gabriel). Dafydd Ducks had a brother called Tommy Walduck Jones and Ducks was derived from Walduck.

Earlier, I wrote that nicknames are seldom, if ever, called to people's faces. Even when said in innocence, that can incur the wrath of the victim, such as in the case of Richard Evans who, for many years, kept the village stores in Borth-y-gest near Porthmadog. When he was a boy, there was a haulage contractor in Porthmadog, where he then lived, known as Evan Gwando.

Gwrando is Welsh for listen, which Evan said frequently, but since he could not say his 'rs', he became known as Evan Gwando. One day he took Richard with him on a trip and on the return home Richard thanked him, calling him Mr Gwando because he thought that was his real name. He received a clout for his insolence and discovered the reason only when he told his mother on returning home.

There are many nicknames, the origins of which are shrouded in mystery. Here are some examples: John Saith Marchog (John Seven Riders or Knights), Stanley Ben Hook, John Points, Ned y Brathwr (Ned the Biter), Dafydd yr Hop (David the Hop, perhaps because he had a limp?), Jack Shake, Johnny Sea Lion, Wilfred Hog, Jonathan Lanky (perhaps because he was tall?), Twm Ffagl (Tom the Torch), Wil Echo, Wil Cyn Dydd (Wil Daybreak?), Dic Tarzan, Rowlands Pioneer, Amy the Well, Wil Pot Eggs, Dei Cratch, Edwin Ceiliog y Gwynt (Edwin the Weather Vane), Jack How Many?, John Three Wheel, Edwin Tweet (long before the days of tweeting), Hywel Peps, Bob Cerrig (Bob Stones), Nita Saith Blewyn (Anita Seven Hairs), Joe Ffliw and Caradog Snogen.

SAYINGS

One of the surest ways to earn a nickname is to have a favourite saying. Most people, however, obviously don't know that they keep on repeating the same word or phrase and more often than not they have the more amusing names.

Twm Absolutely was a south Wales councillor who said absolutely after almost everything. That name could apply to hundreds of people today as it is frequently said by those being interviewed on radio or televison. Exactly Jones falls into the same category as does John Ie Ie (John Yes Yes).

Jones Balloon was given the name after the visit of a VIP to the factory where he was a foreman. Shortly before the visitor arrived at his section, he implored his men: "Now boys, whatever you do, don't let me down." Glyn Prediction constantly prefaced his sentences with: "I'll tell you what will happen boys."

John Evans Urban Powers, who was a councillor in a rural part of North Wales, continually referred to the threat of urban powers, and another councillor was known as Dai Committee because he always moved that the committees on which he served, or the full council, should "go into committee" (secret session) whenever he thought the Press should be excluded. Harry Point of Order was a councillor who continually interrupted debates by raising points of order. To the amusement of his colleagues, his interruptions were hardly ever ruled as points of order.

In years gone by, when chapel worshippers were carried away with the earnestness of the preacher intoning prayers, many a man would shout out Amen or Halleluja. Thus we have John Amen from the old county of Meirionnydd and Jones Hallelujah from a valley in Gwent.

Dai Piano was so-called, not for his musical ability, but for cadging cigarettes. As he helped himself from the packets of long-suffering friends, they would ask: "No cigarettes, Dai?" and he would reply: "No, I've left them at home on the piano." A similar tight-fisted Carmarthenshire man was known as Owen-One-I-Got because whenever he was asked for a sweet or cigarette he would say: "Sorry, only one I got," before putting the packet or bag away.

Now Taw'r Diawl lived in north Wales. Now is a corruption of Owen and Taw'r Diawl means 'be quiet you devil'. Apparently, when he wanted to have his say, which was often, he used this expression.

Dai Foot and Mouth was a Llanelli rugby supporter who, with a voice like thunder, always shouted at charging forwards: "Feet! Feet!" Hop It was the name given to an Aberystwyth teacher because after giving a pupil a talking-to, he would always end by saying: "Now hop it." Peter Cloudy lived in Clwyd and greeted everyone each day by saying "Cloudy today" no matter what the weather.

Many people go through life being cheerful... or miserable. In the latter category was an Aberystwyth baker named Dai Llond Bol (Dai Bellyful). People who are fed up often say in Welsh: "Dw i wedi cael llond bol" – I've had a bellyful of it – and Dai was constantly saying this. One man was called Elfed Ooh There's Lovely, not because he used the phrase, but because his wife was always saying it.

I have come across only two women in this category and they both lived in north Wales. Mrs Jones Come By Here was so-named because that is what she said to her children when she wanted to talk to them, and Mary Toodle-oo always said goodbye in this way.

A postman in a mid Wales town got his nickname, not for what he said, but for what he wrote. Because Welsh was his first language, his English was poor, to say the least. He wanted to write on an envelope that the recipient had died, so he wrote just two words: "She Dead." From then on he was Tommy She Dead.

Wili One-a-One (Willy One and One) lived in north Wales many years ago and collecetd a penny a week from the townspeople for the Rachabites Friendly Society. When counting from the book to pay out, he would say dozens of times: "one-a-one-a-one-a-one-a-one-a-one…"

Dic Wireless was always saying: "Heard it on the wireless" and Eric Aros Funud (Eric Wait a Minute) used to start nearly every sentence with "Wait a minute…" Bili Drws (Billy Door) always sat in the same seat in his local and whenever anyone came though the door, no matter what the weather, he would turn round and say: "Cau drws" – Shut the door. Emrys Cariad (Emrys Sweetheart) earned the name because he always called the ladies "Cariad".

Twm Rafferty sounds like a real name but it's a nickname and a corruption of "r'un fath â ti" (the same as you), which was his favourite saying when someone offered to buy him a drink. William Jones Dewch i Mewn (William Jones Come In) regularly shouted that when someone called at his house, while Johnny Call Again was a Caernarfon jeweller who always said to his customers as they left his shop: "Thank you very much, call again."

John Hen Lol (John Nonsense) often said "hen lol" during arguments with friends, and Tommy Uncle John was given the name because as a boy he used to say: "My Uncle John did this" or "My Uncle John did that."

A north Wales man who swore a lot was known as Dic Rhegi (Dick Swearing) and into the same category fell Harry Bugger and Twm Bloody. A man who started work in a north Wales coalmine did not swear, but his favourite expression was "Man alive!" – so he was called Harry Man Alive. He had not been in the pit long before he was swearing with the rest of them, but the original name stuck.

CAUTIOUS SAYINGS

Nicknames can also arise in certain circumstances. Students have brought in a saying: "He got a Desmond." Any student getting a lower second class degree – a 2-2 – is said to have been given a Desmond after Archbishop Desmond Tutu.

Getting Brahms and Liszt is an old bit of Cockney rhyming slang for getting really drunk, but a new description has come in after the name of Oskar Schindler, the heroic German immortalised in the film *Schindler's List*. Anyone being drunk and incapable is said to have got "absolutely schindlers".

Many people, knowing the habit of giving nicknames, do their utmost to avoid earning one. But it is usually talking about nicknames that catches them out.

Take, for instance, a man named Evans who moved to south Wales from the Midlands and was warned before leaving about the giving of nicknames. When he started work in Wales, he said: "Don't worry about me, I'm too clever to be caught like that." From that moment he was known as Clever Evans. In north Wales, a slate quarry worker, knowing the nickname habit, said: "They'll have to be early birds to catch me." So they called him Jack Early Bird. In the same part of the world, a miner joining a pit told his workmates: "Bydda i'n ddiniwed fel yr oen" (I'll be as innocent as a lamb), so he was called Twm yr Oen (Tom the Lamb).

When Englishman William Davies went to work at a slate quarry in Blaenau Ffestiniog, he said on being told that probably eventually he would be given a nickname: "I'll always be on the look out to see that they don't give me one." Sure enough, he became Will Look Out!

Some people are concerned not to be given a cruel or ridiculous nickname. Such a one was Dai Thomas who moved to work at a north Wales quarry. When the foreman heard his name he said: "We've got too many Thomases already, man. You'll have to have a nickname." He looked hard, hoping to detect a squint, big feet or ears, or some disfigurement. Fearing some dreadful name, Dai said with dignity: "Well, if you have to give me a bloody name, give me something substantial." So he became Dai Substantial.

A similar story is told about a north Wales miner who moved to a pit in south Wales. He told his workmates rather pompously: "Now see here boys, I know you are deciding on a nickname for me, but I hope it won't be too disputatious." The result? Yes, you've guessed it – Disputatious Evans.

SPORT

Sport provides many nicknames. The career of the late Mervyn Davies, the massive No. 8 and captain of Wales, was cut tragically short when he had to have brain surgery after collapsing during a game. He was affectionately known to all rugby supporters as Merve the Swerve. Cliff Morgan, another great Welsh rugby hero who also captained his country and later became a top BBC television executive, was known as Morgan the Organ because of his great love of organ music.

Perhaps the three most famous Welsh rugby players with nicknames come from the Pontypool club. Charlie Faulkner was known as Mr Indestructable and Graham Price as Lionhead. Bobby Windsor was Duke, probably because of his surname, which may be true, but one story is that when he was first selected for the Wales international squad, he was so thrilled and delighted that he wanted to give a good impression. He turned up for training in a smart suit and a collar and tie, while the others arrived in casual clothes. Billy Hooker played in that position for a west Wales club and Tommy Lock was the lock forward in another team.

Wales international footballer Arfon Griffiths, who had a spell with Arsenal but who spent most of his playing days with Wrexham before becoming their manager, was known as The Little General for his skill as captain of the team and for marshalling his players during matches.

At one time the Wrexham club had a chaplain and when the Rev. Paul Brown was appointed, team coach Joey Jones, the former Liverpool, Chelsea and Wrexham player, nicknamed him Charlie Chaplain.

Joey has given nicknames to many players in the clubs he has been associated with. Typical was that given to Kevin Russell who played for Wrexham and a number of other clubs. Because of the type of haircut he had when he arrived for training one day, Joey called him Rooster and that name stuck so that whenever Russell scored, the Wrexham crowd chanted "Rooster, Rooster!"

John Jones was a good amateur footballer in Blaenau Ffestiniog and people said he had a shot like a cannon ball, so he became John Jones Cannon. His son was not a footballer but he inherited the name Dai Cannon. Another footballer from Wrexham was called Dai Feet.

Perhaps the man who gained the most publicity as an international football referee was Welshman Clive Thomas. He became known as Clive the Book throughout the land because he was a strict disciplinarian on the field and made a name for himself by giving out many yellow or red cards, putting the players' names in his black book.

FOREIGN COUNTRIES

Anyone who has worked abroad or even in some cases claims to have done so, usually has an appropriate nickname. An example is the man who went to America for a short visit and returned with an American accent – he immediately became Ted Yank. Teddy Bombay from Aberystwyth served in India while in the army and Davies Hong Kong, from the same town, was a civil servant who used to work in that colony.

Robin Shanghai was reputed to have been to that Chinese city and Bob Far East served there while in the forces. Wipers Evans came from Llanelli and had fought in the First World War at Ypres which British Tommies called Wipers. A posthumous nickname was given to a Bethesda man killed in the Dardanelles in the same war and he was always referred to as Bob Dardanelles.

The Spanish Civil War produced Twm Spain, and Jack Russia was said to be a communist from Abertridwr.

Humour comes through in many cases, such as in Himalaya Hugh who was Mr H. Hugh Jones, headmaster of Llangollen County School in the 1920s. He taught geography and had been in India during the First World War, so that whenever he gave a lesson, he could never resist mentioning the Himalayas.

FAMILIES

The head of a big family, or a member of a big family, is always liable to be nicknamed. One Cardiganshire family was known as Plant Golau Dydd (Daylight Children) because their father worked permanent nights! Will Population fathered 13 children and Jones Channel Fleet received his nickname because someone once said of him: "Duw, he's got enough children to man the Channel Fleet." Moi Six lived in north Wales. Moi is the shortened form for Maurice and he was the sixth child in the family.

Another way of giving a nickname is after a mother, grandmother or wife and many an English tourist in a pub or shop has been taken aback when a local has been referred to as, for example, George Peggy (George the husband of Peggy).

Jac Betsi was named after his mother and a fuller version was found in another part of north Wales in Wil Bachgen Mari (Will Mary's son). *Nain* is the north Wales Welsh word for grandmother and a boy brought up by his grandmother was always known as Tomi Nain. Wil Bodo was brought up by his aunt (*bodo* being the Welsh for aunt), and so was Jack Auntie Liz. Harold Jackie Jack was the son of John Roberts who was the son of Jack Jenkin Roberts.

EVEN THE FAMOUS

Even the famous do not escape the net. Former Ardwyn Grammar School, Aberystwyth, pupil John Morris, was MP for Aberavon and was a former Welsh Secretary in a Labour Government. He once used a Government helicopter to take him from Aberystwyth to Bala for a political meeting and was criticised for doing so. Wags immediately gave him the name of Chopper Morris. His good schoolfriend, now Lord Elystan Morgan, former MP for Cardiganshire and a former Under-Secretary at the Home Office who eventually became a High Court Judge, was called Elastic Morgan by the non Welsh-speaking pupils in our school.

Sir David Maxwell Fyfe, later Lord Kilmuir, visited University College of Wales, Aberystwyth when he was Home Secretary in the 1950s. The students nicknamed him Dai Bananas after Fyffes bananas.

Former Labour Leader and Leader of the Opposition, now Baron Kinnock of Bedwellty, and his wife Glenys, a one-time MEP and now a Life Peer, were known as The Power and the Glory when they were students in Cardiff. This arose, it is said, because Glenys was the power behind the throne while Neil enjoyed the glory of being President of the Students' Union. During a General Election years later, the Tories attempted to belittle him by calling him the Welsh Windbag and Boyo. Welsh Labour supporters, in return, called Welsh Secretary, David Hunt, Dai Jackanory, a teller of tales.

One of the cleverest nicknames given in Parliament was that allocated to Welshman John Stradling Thomas who, as Deputy Chief Whip, was affectionately known as Angel Delight. This was because when he entered Parliament in 1970, in a very short space of time he became a junior in the Whip's office, which made him an instant whip like the dessert of that name. Undoubtedly the politician with the nationally-known nickname was Liberal Prime Minister David Lloyd George – the Welsh Wizard.

SOME OF MY FAVOURITES

Finally, among all the nicknames about which I have written, these are some of my favourites.

One of the heroes of the ill-fated Battle of Arnhem in the last war was Flt. Lt. David Lord of Wrexham, who according to the citation was awarded the Victoria Cross for his "supreme valour and self-sacrifice". His bravery saw both Allied and German soldiers stop their fierce fighting to watch in awe as he brought his plane down single-handed having ordered his crew to bale out so that he could crash-land away from the town. Sadly, he was killed in doing so. Throughout his air force career he had been known to his comrades as Lumme Lord because that was what he said instead of swearing.

As a former brass bandsman, I have collected quite a few nicknames in that field, such as Wil Solo Horn, Wil John Cornet and Bill Bass who played the B flat bass in the Aberystwyth British Legion Silver Band with me. My favourite, however, was a very original one, Glyn Go There, Come Back – generally shortened to Glyn Go – who was a trombone player in a Rhondda band!

In north Wales, quarrymen were required to put their initials on the pillars they had quarried, so Dafydd Owen Jones simply put O.J. Ever after he was known as Dafydd Ooja, a corruption of O.J.

Another example of no matter how hard you try to keep

an incident quiet, the details will eventually leak out and the inevitable nickname will follow. Typical was Ned Bekloo (Ned Bakerloo) who was a north Wales man who got lost on the London Underground. John Mynydd (John Mountain) also got lost one day while walking on a mountain not far from his home.

Les Lens was a patient in a mental hospital who believed he was being poisoned and used to look at his food and under his plate with a magnifying glass.

On a happier note, a long name was given to a north Wales family known as Teulu Fi, Fo a Fynta (the family of Me, Him and the Other One). The nickname referred to a father and his two sons who never bought drinks in a pub for anyone except themselves. When ordering drinks they would say in Welsh, "Un i fi, un iddo fo ac un i fynta" ("one for me, one for him and one for the other one").

Dai Mikado was the name given to an Aberdare man who played the character in the Gilbert and Sullivan opera and Bob Sinatra was a good singer who impersonated Frank Sinatra, but sang only in pubs after he had had a good intake of drink.

If I may end on a personal note, my wife Carol who lived in Wolverhampton as a child, often went with her mother to visit her grandmother in Tanygrisiau, near Blaenau Ffestiniog. She was always referred to by the villagers as Hogan Fach Lizzie Sal (the little girl of Lizzie, daughter of Sal).

I am often asked if I have been given a nickname. Only one – as far as I know! – and that was when I was at school. A former Mayor of Aberystwyth was known as Tubby Price and his wife who lived near to me started calling me Ches. Her son and daughter were at our school, so they most probably took the name to school and passed it around and that is what I became known as – to my face at least!

Earlier I said that the habit of nicknaming is as prevalent today as it ever was. After reading this book, don't think you are immune. Remember the stories of Clever Evans, Jack Early Bird and Wil Look Out… that is, if you haven't already been nicknamed!

Author biography

Les Chamberlain was born in Aberystwyth and after starting his journalistic career on the *Cambrian News* there, he worked in Nottingham before moving to Coventry for 20 years, working on the *Birmingham Mail* and then the *Coventry Evening Telegraph* where he was deputy news editor for eight years. He moved to Wrexham in 1978, joining the staff of the *Wrexham Leader* and later transferred to the sister paper, the *Evening Leader*, where he was deputy news editor. He took early retirement in 1994 but continued to work as a freelance journalist. He is married with a son who is a journalist in India, a daughter and three grandsons.

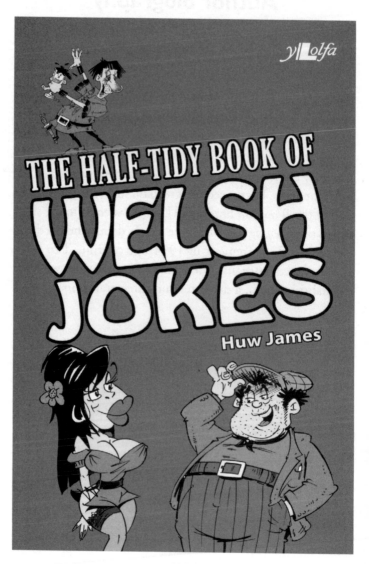

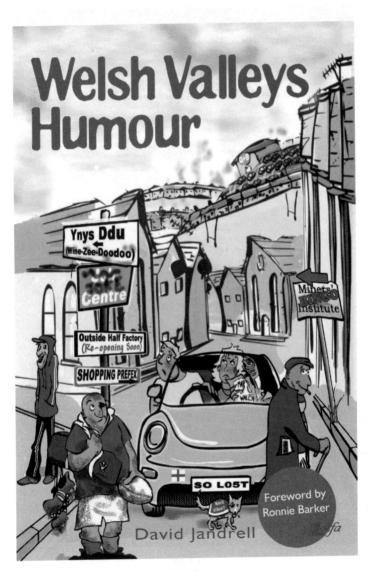

Welsh Valleys Humour

Ynys Ddu
(Wine-Zee-Doodoo)

JOB
Centre

Outside Half Factory
(Re-opening Soon)

SHOPPING PREFEX

Miners'
BINGO
Institute

MAP
OF
WALES

SO L05T

Foreword by
Ronnie Barker

David Jandrell

£3.95

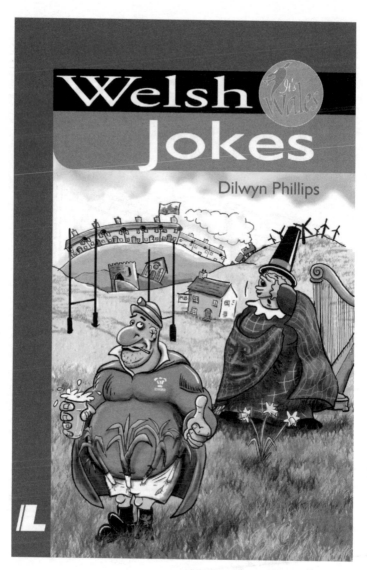

Welsh Jokes

Jokes

Dilwyn Phillips

£3.95

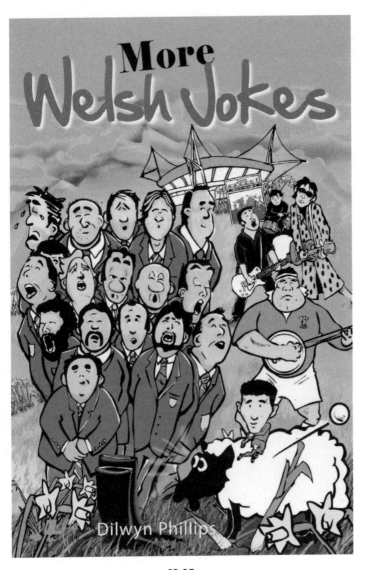

More
Welsh Jokes

Dilwyn Phillips

£3.95

Welsh Nicknames is just one of a whole range of publications from Y Lolfa. For a full list of books currently in print, send now for your free copy of our new full-colour catalogue. Or simply surf into our website

www.ylolfa.com

for secure on-line ordering.

TALYBONT CEREDIGION CYMRU SY24 5HE
e-mail ylolfa@ylolfa.com
website www.ylolfa.com
phone (01970) 832 304
fax 832 782